Angela's Rainbow

Angela's Rainbow

MICHAEL JOHNSON

Written by
Lisa Tuttle

Paper Tiger

A Dragon's World Ltd Imprint

Dragon's World Ltd
Limpsfield
Surrey RH8 0DY
Great Britain

Designed by Steve Henderson

Hardback: ISBN 0 905895 74 6

Printed in Spain
D. L. : BI - 1.108 - 1983
E. Belgas, S. L.
Emilio Arrieta, 2 - Bilbao - 12

When I was a child I was magic and did not know it. I came into the world with my eyes wide open, alarmed by what I saw. Reality, they called it, and it was too solid to be disbelieved. I had memories of another life, other worlds, but they told me there was no other.

Still I hoped, searching after wonders, believing in possibilities. Believing that, in time, the ordinary would blossom before my eyes and fill my soul with the scent of miracles. Stones would give tongue, white birds lift me to the moon where, in a castle of jade and carnelian, a handsome prince waited, sword drawn and gleaming silver in the earth-light.

An angel came to me in my dreams: a beautiful being with the body of a woman, wisdom and passion flaming from haunted eyes. Her hands, where they stroked, turned my body to water and silk. Mouth to mouth she spoke to me, pouring a voice rich and hot as wine, cool and soothing as milk, down my eager throat. I grew drunk on her songs, and fed on tales of far-away, of the darkness behind the stars and the blazing glory human eyes never see.

One night my mother found me, naked as on the day of my birth, spinning in the centre of the floor, eyes tightly shut and mouth open wide to receive the angel-speech, humming low in my throat and laughing for sheer joy. When she woke me, I told her about the angel, wondering at the fear in her face. She hugged me tightly, and wept, and in the morning she took me to a quiet, chilly office where a quiet, chilly man asked me questions about my dreams. I saw him often after that, and he drew my dreams from me. The angel stopped coming. My mother stopped weeping. I watched television with the family instead of sitting alone in my room. I became good at mathematics, no longer distracted by the colours and the music behind the numbers. My childhood was over.

But in maturity there were consolations. There were, above all, the pleasures of the flesh. There were men. What did I care for the singing and the glowing of the stars when the hands of men were stroking me into life?

There was one man in particular: I thought he was my longed-for prince, for I awakened to his kiss. He made me real, I thought, as if he were the artist and I rough clay: my breasts swelled to fill his cupped hands, the curve of my hips obeyed his caress as he shaped me. I let him dress me in white, for I was his bride, his child, a virginal sacrifice led to the altar of life. I looked into my lover's eyes and saw that I was beautiful. Love was sweeter and more intoxicating than the speech of angels, and it kept me dizzy and content. For a while, that was enough.

But deep within me was a fragment, a shard of memory bright and insubstantial as the feather from an angel's wing, a confused dream-idea of something else. And, like the grain of sand which in the oyster turns to pearl, it rubbed at my life, becoming more solid with the passage of time. My lover did not understand. He thought I was childish. But he was the ignorant, innocent one, to be content with so little, to be unaware of possibilities just beyond his grasp. I realised it was not myself I saw reflected in his eyes, but merely an image of me, his creation, which he loved.

I ran away from him to find myself, like a child running in search of fairyland, or seeking the pot of gold at the end of the rainbow, against all adult wisdom and advice. Love was not enough. The pleasure that I felt, shuddering in his arms, was merely the shadow of something greater. Our two bodies struggled to become one, but they could never succeed.

Trying to find the answer, looking for something greater than myself, I gave myself to strangers: powerful men with curling black hair and strong white teeth, beautiful men with painted faces, men who smelled of sweat and men who dripped money, men who murmured in other languages and men who swore at me, men who swept me off my feet and men who paid me for my favours, men who tied me down with silken ropes, men as brutal and stupid as animals, and men so delicate they broke and melted in my hands. There were women, too, sisters who searched, like me, for something they could not name, something more powerful than love, more real than this reality.

I found ecstasy and regret on silken sheets in perfumed, candle-lit rooms; in a rocking wooden boat that stank of fish; in cheap hotels high above the sound of traffic against the hard, stone walls of ancient alleyways; on grassy, sunlit shores near the sound of the thundering sea – and always, at the core, it was the same experience. It was not enough. None of these strangers could give me what my soul craved.

Despairing, I turned my back on men and women and sought my fate in solitude, in work, in art, in travel. In search of my true, my spiritual home, I left the urban America where I had been born and followed the trail of my ancestors, backwards across the ocean. In the old world there was still peace, still the possibility of a simple life close to the soil. Briefly I luxuriated in the serenity of nature: sunlight warm on my bare arms, the rich, heady fragrance of growing things, the melody of birdsong in counterpoint to the distant lowing of cattle. It was an ancient, beautiful pattern, but it did not include me. I could not find a home in these neatly tilled and tended fields—they did not hold the answer to the secret of my life.

There were others like me in the world, dissatisfied and always moving, outcasts by blood or by choice. I thought I might find my home among them, outside the terrible machinery of civilisation. But the stateless were yet victims of the State: punished for breaking rules not their own, hounded, herded, rounded up, murdered in wars they neither caused nor fought. I was not one of them. Their dark, haunted eyes looked past me to ponder the problems of survival.
I fled the ravages of humankind.
Somewhere there must be primeval forces unaffected by the puny efforts of Man: a deeper, more permanent reality.
Alone and on foot I travelled into the cold, high mountains at the roof of the world, terrain which had not changed since the beginning of time. Perhaps the ancient gods still sat there in judgement. Beyond the mountains was a vast, scorched desert, as bleak and empty as the end of time. Here, with nothing but rock and sand and sun, I could not be distracted. I must face my self.

The desert gave me the key. One day I saw a small miracle, a rainbow.

Refraction and reflection, sunlight transformed to pure colour by water droplets invisible in the air—the scientific explanation. But the air rasping my lungs and abrading my skin was hot and dry as a dragon's breath, holding not even the memory of moisture. Without water there could be no refraction, no reflection, no rainbow. Yet I saw it, a brilliant arc across the barren earth in the hard, blue sky.

Bifrost, the rainbow bridge which connected the home of the gods to this world. I imagined stepping on to it. I could almost feel the colours swirling softly, warmly about my legs, rising almost to my knees in a delicious, perfumed cloud of pastels, yet still solid beneath my feet, the solidity of primary colours, basic and unyielding, supporting me as I climbed. Could I climb all the way to Asgard? Only the gods could cross Bifrost; only gods and heroes.

A warrior God's mighty bow, set in the clouds as a sign. Not only a bridge, but a promise. To me? There was no one else in this lonely place to see it.

Perhaps this was what I had been seeking all along. As in some ritual I cast off my clothes and turned my back on my old life, on the world. I walked towards the rainbow, dedicating myself to it, prepared to face whatever it showed me, to follow wherever it led.

Harsh, brilliant day was covered by the gentle cloak of night, and my rainbow faded, then vanished from sight. I was not alarmed; I did not feel abandoned.

Heaven's bridge is not shattered by the passage of the sun, and I knew the rainbow still glowed, still marked a steady path across the sky, even though it was now invisible, to be seen only by the inward eye.

All through the night I gazed at the distant, serene face of the moon, feeling her tidal pull at my blood. She was my mother, the sun my father. I felt at one with the rocks around me, ancient, massive and still, and I beat to the slow, steady pulse of the Earth. Everything was alive, and I was part of that life, no longer cut off from it by trivialities, no longer estranged by my own restlessness.

I was growing, as mountains and as plants do, but in my own time, in my own way. At last, nurtured in this new-found peace, something new might emerge. I felt it within me, something with the heat and dazzling brightness of a star. A new awareness, a new power. And yet not really new, for it had always been inside me, invisible as the rainbow in the night sky, but just as real.

Like the moth within the chrysalis, like the chick within the egg, something was struggling inside me to be free.

Wings beat hard within my chest, against my rib cage. I choked on words in a language I did not understand. Plangent music keened through my veins. Visions of another world seared my eyelids. I tried to move and could not. What was I? Where?

A familiar voice, loved since childhood but now nearly forgotten, spoke in my ear and soothed my panic. I did not understand the words, but I knew the tone. The angel from my dreams was near me now, protecting me, welcoming me.

I felt her touch me, with hands like sunlight and air, and her kisses flowed over me like water. Still I could not see her, but I knew that all was well. Patience. Soon I would soar above the earth, set free. Soon all she had told me in my youth would come true. I would no longer be trapped by my body or the accidents of time or place.

The ember inside me glowed red-hot, ready to consume and liberate.

I was not alone. I never had been. There was someone else inside me.
She was waking now, after a sleep of years. Always she had been within me,
buried deep, dreaming deep beneath my thoughts and fears, my experiences,
the persona I showed to the world. She was me and yet she was not-me. She was
far more than the simple woman I thought I was, and she had undergone many
births and burials in many different bodies. She might have gone on sleeping,
unnoticed, inside me until my death, but something – the angel? the rainbow?
my own restless yearnings? – had summoned her to the surface again.
She yawned and stirred, flexing long unused muscles. She opened my eyes and
looked out at the world – my world, now hers again. She moved my hands over
my body, delighting in its youth and firmness.

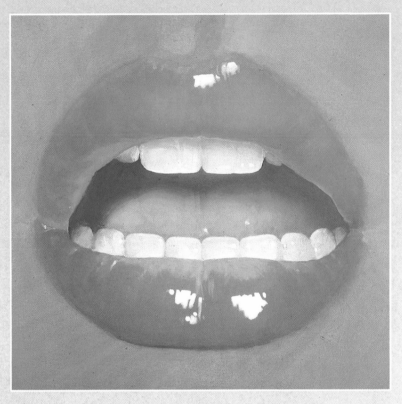

She danced and ran, exulting in the feel of
the hard earth slapping against my bare feet and the
dry, gritty air against my smooth skin. She was old,
old, centuries old, and it was good to be young and
beautiful again.

My mind was flooded with her experiences,
memories, sensations, desires. I was overwhelmed
by her presence, by her power which I knew now had
always been mine to call upon.

She opened my mouth and she spoke.

We said: "I am."

How long had I slept? My whole life, to this moment, was but a dream, a restless, discontented sleep. Now I remembered who I was.

I was born of the meeting between Earth and Sky. I was the daughter of the Thunder and the Sea. When lightning split the oak tree, there stood I, revealed. I was the Morning Star, the Daughter of the Moon. I had many names. The children of Man and Woman called me Goddess. They named me Ishtar, Astarte, Isis, Rhiannon, Aganju, Tiamat, Sarasvati, Aruru, Demeter and Aphrodite.

For a Long time I ruled, Queen of Heaven and of Earth. I had many consorts, many worshippers, many children, but as time passed my people turned their faces from me and forgot.

Forgotten I might be, but not gone. I did not vanish any more than do the stars when the sun shines. The ways of the Goddess were lost, but I was born and born again in the body of a woman. I did not remember who I had been. Only a restlessness remained, a divine discontent which drove me from one identity to another, searching for something I could not name.

Now I had returned, and the old knowledge, the power, was waiting for me. I listened to the tale the thunder told. I felt lightning crackle through my arteries, electrifying me. Other languages hissed and whispered in my ears, and when I moved I danced to the ancient, powerful rhythms of the universe, in tune once more, at home.

I rediscovered the world, and it welcomed me back like an ardent lover. My skin glowed beneath the sun's kisses, greedily absorbing its warmth. I pressed myself against the earth, kissing it in gratitude for the life it gave me.
Testing my powers, I called down rain, and drank it in as eagerly as the parched soil. Droplets and streams of water I wore like finery, wanting no other jewels, and I turned my face towards it, glorying in the wetness.

I sought out other sources of power, travelling to the sacred places of the earth, spots where the ancients, worshipping me, had erected rough pillars of stone. The great sarsens, rooted in earth-magic, reached up boldly, to call down the magic of the stars. I stood among them, and let the forces of time and place be channelled through me. And I felt it charge me, vivify me, stirring me body and soul. The embers of passion flamed to life.

The world shimmered and dissolved around me. I saw it through water, through glass, through smoke and flame, and then it was gone. I was in limbo, hanging on the edge. From the void I heard angelic voices, the singing of those never born, the voices of the old gods, calling me back. For a moment I longed to go, but then blackness, soft and warm, enveloped my body.

Night kissed my eyes shut and drew me into his embrace. Night, my brother, my first lover. We were twins, born of Chaos, two children clinging together in terror of the emptiness around us. Naked, new and innocent, we reached out to each other.

With small, searching hands I explored his maleness and he my female mysteries. We kept each other warm in the long, cold eternity before time began. We had no words for what we did, but the Greeks named us Erebus and Nyx, and from our union Eros was born.

But we were not innocent now. As I felt my brother's hands moving on me I trembled with anticipation, my skin quickened in a response that was half pleasurable, half fearful. I thought of Night's mysteries, the secrets he must know, the cruelties as well as the pleasures which are hidden in the darkness. Yet, assaulted by his stroking, probing hands, his mouth on mine, I had no choice but to respond.

Always at the heart of darkness there is light;
the night contains the day. As I caressed the
enveloping blackness, my stroking fingers
drew forth a flare of colour, the blazing
curve of my rainbow.
It slipped beneath my hand to slide itself
along my body, warming me with burning
brightness as it rippled and coiled about me.
My rainbow: not a bridge or a bow or a
pathway this time, but the celestial snake.
Dan Ayido Hwedo the Africans called him:
the magnificent serpent who circles the
world, drawing its many parts and people
together in cosmic unity.
I gave myself up to the rhythms of the snake,
letting it guide me. Coloured scales roiled
and flowed beneath and around me,
carrying me away beyond thought, bringing
me to wholeness and completion.

Colours moved through me, over and under me like flowing water, hot and cold, sheer sensation. I tasted yellow and red upon my tongue: I inhaled scarlet and violet. The colours were behind my eyes and in my brain. They licked my skin like a rough-tongued cat, then enveloped me with smooth, silken coolness. Blue and green caressed me to sleep; orange stung me awake. Flaming shades and liquid hues covered me, filled me, inspired my senses. Matter liquified, evaporated, became the chromatic prism. I arched my back, or it arched me, and I *was* the rainbow.

I was the bridge that leads from dull human habit to the ecstasy of the gods, and I knew them all, all the gods and heroes who marched or danced or strolled across me. Until the day of Ragnarok, when the thundering hooves, the heavy battle-chariots rattling across my gleaming arc were too much for me to bear and I shattered beneath their assault, falling back to earth in a rain of multi-coloured light.

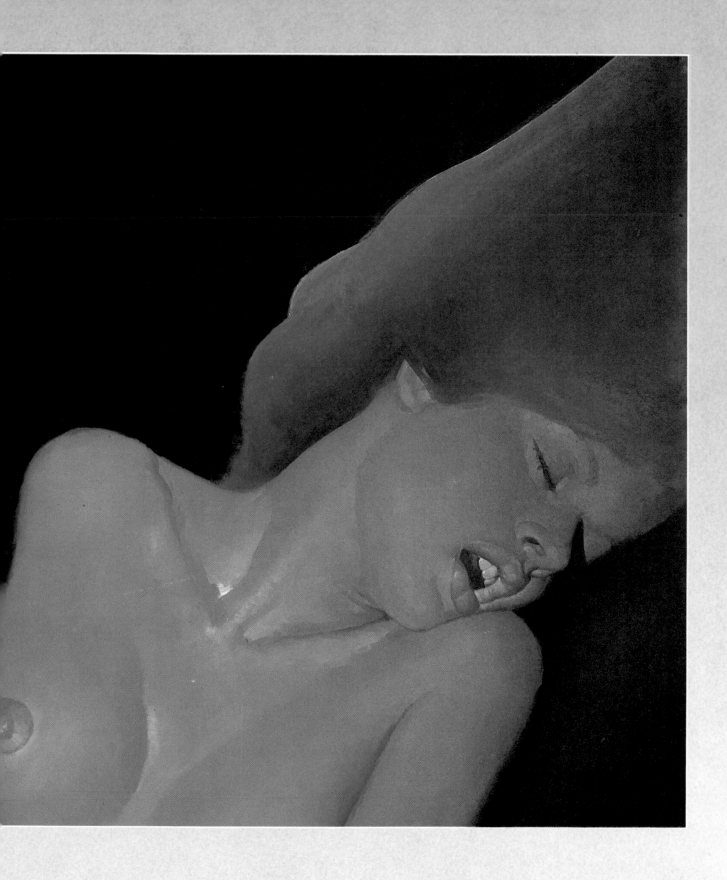

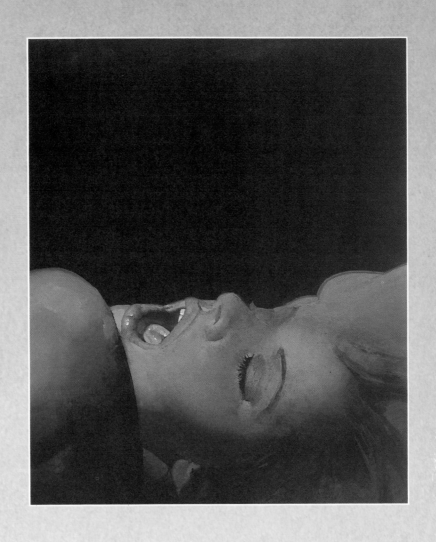

But Heimdall, Guardian of the Rainbow, noble Lord of Light, gathered up my pieces in his powerful hands. And on the morning after Ragnarok, in the desolate silence that follows battle, he rebuilt me, shaped me into a woman of flesh and blood and set me down upon the land.

My thoughts were always and only for him; I yearned for his love as a flower grows towards the sun. Mortals should seek mortal lovers, my father told me, the love of a god would destroy me. So he locked me away to preserve my treasure for a human husband. Yet I dreamed of burning. Kneeling in my tower, gazing at the stained-glass windows recalling his eyes, I prayed for immolation. And he came to me in a deluge of light, a storm of gold, scarlet and crimson. I felt him warm upon my lips and opened my mouth to let him drink from me. His tongue sent fire coursing along my veins. Dazzled by his radiance, I opened my eyes, determined to see him.

He had the appearance of a man: huge, red-bearded, handsome, powerful. The sight of him stirred my desire. Not caring whether he was god or man, I offered him my body. When he took me, I knew which he was.

At his touch, my clothes ignited and burned away. His hands, taking possession of my nakedness, branded me with his sign, and his kisses blazed like live coals against my tender flesh.

Despite the pain I pressed myself against him, seeking more, trying to travel through the agony to the brilliance I sensed beyond. When he entered me the ecstasy was unendurable. I burst into flames. I was consumed.

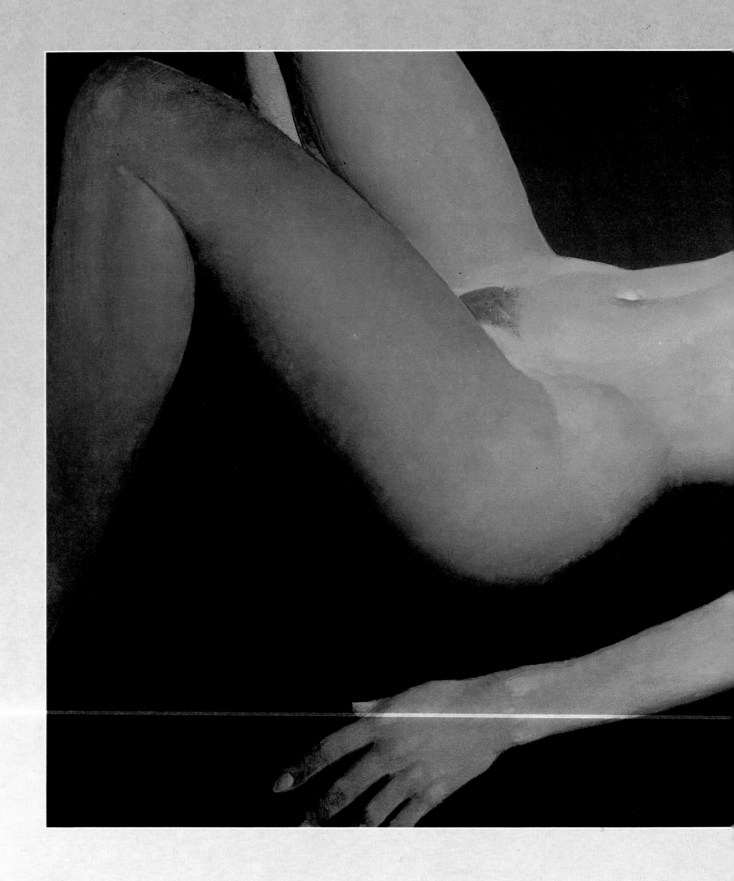

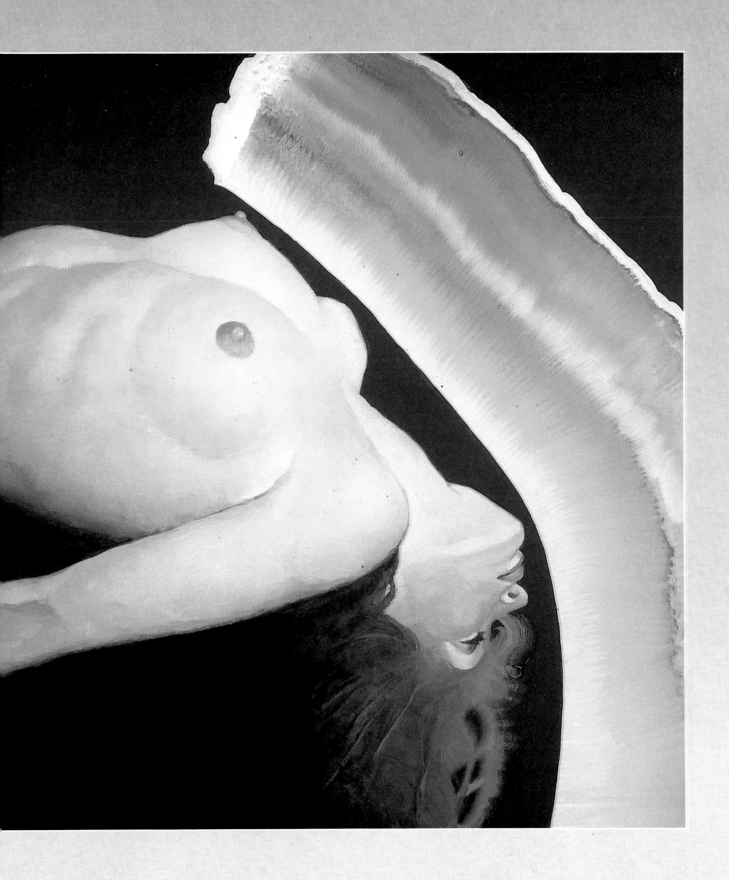

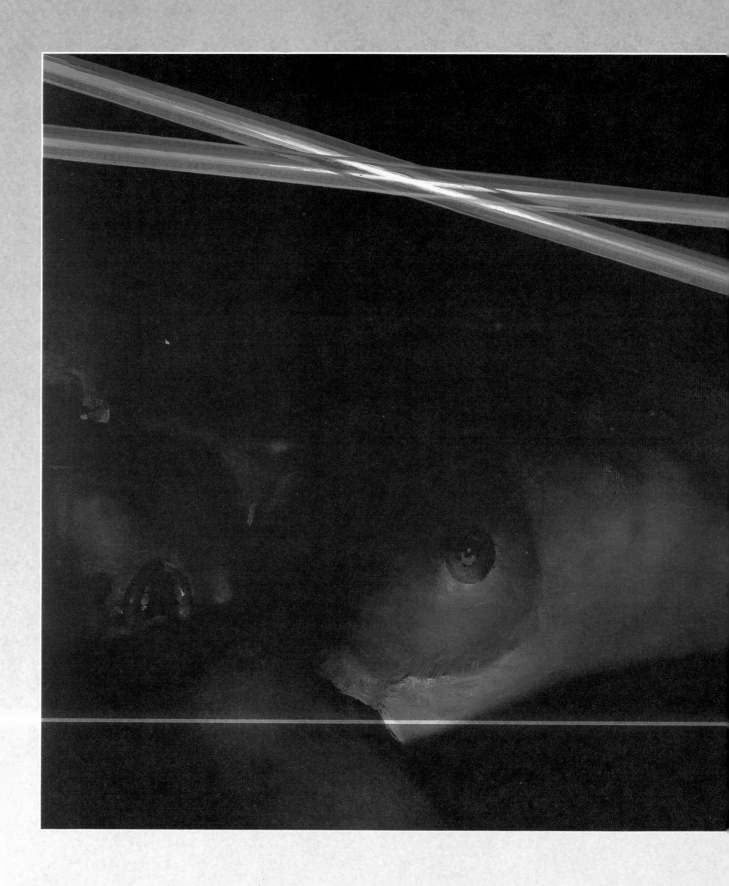

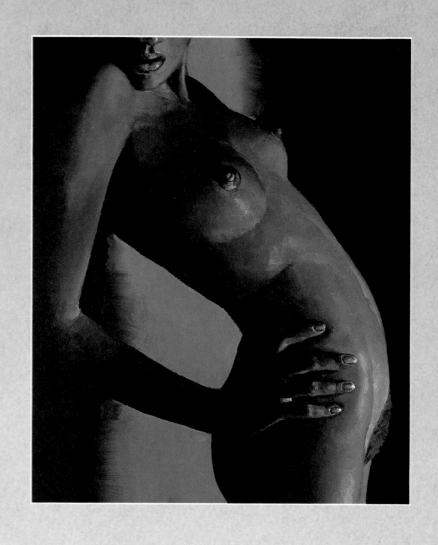

My body became the earth. I felt the multitude of beings that moved upon me, tilling and tending and worshipping, loving and hating, all life, all potential. Above, the sky caressed me, stroking me with sunlight, kissing me with rain.

I boiled and teemed with life, with a magical force. I could feel it within me, feel it throbbing with my every inhalation.

It was a dragon in a cavern deep inside; it was a serpent coiled at the base of my spine. It was my servant to command, a powerful, magical beast, and a part of me. It awaited my decision, my recognition. It waited for the moment of release.

The time had come. I let out my breath. I said the word.

I felt the serpent uncoiling. My body shuddered, my back arched, cracking with the fearful, painful, wonderful glory. Lightning seared my spine as the great snake unwound, stretching out inside me, moving up towards the light.

The serpent filled me, stretching my body to its limits, until I could no longer contain it. The agony was fearful; I knew I was dying. And still desire drove me: along with the pain was a reckless, ecstatic urge for more. More than I could bear. My body split open. I exploded into colours. I was the serpent bursting free; I was the rainbow snake, flying.

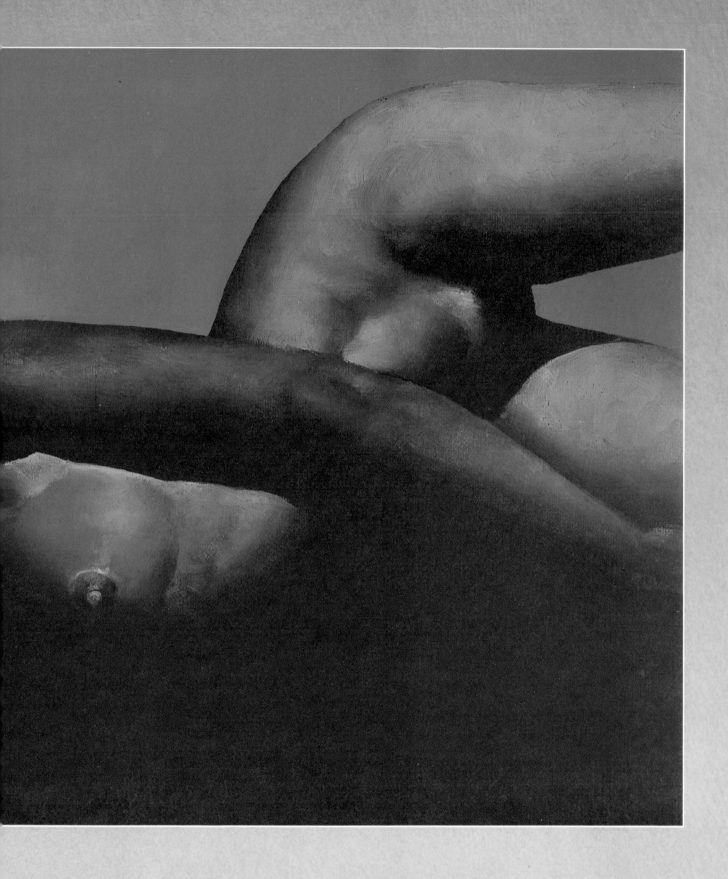

I was colour. I was sound. I was radiance. I was light.
I had no form. I was pure energy.
Waves of sensation washed over me, ripples from a
carmine sea. Outside time, outside space. Blood-
warm and throbbing. I was the universe, and I was
nothingness.
Through Chaos, through darkness and light, into
being. Vast formless clouds embraced me, merging
with me, then giving birth to me. Slowly I became
myself again. I knew the boundaries of my body. I
remembered my name.
I became aware of my surroundings. I knew where I
was, now. The cracked soil of the desert crumbled to
powder beneath the pressure of my hands and
knees: I was sprawling on the earth, gazing at the
blue vault of the sky and the emptiness around me,
exhausted.
Slowly, uncertainly, I rose on shaky legs, feeling the
frailty of my body. I ached. I felt drained and empty.
My body still reverberated with the force that had
shaken me, but was now only a hollow shell. The
power had gone. I had been used and then cast aside.
But what had used me? I remembered the serpent
coiled inside me, filling me, lashing out of my body to
freedom, setting *me* free. Because I was the snake.
And the power was mine.
Certainty kindled deep within, filling me with the
warmth of triumph. My aching body was forgotten. I
knew my power, and I wasn't empty any more.
With one powerful kick against the hard ground, I
sent myself flying into the thin desert air. I surged
higher, leaping free of the bonds of gravity, passing
out of the chains of time, aiming for the glowing heart
of the sun.
I swam through soft, cool clouds into blinding light. I
gulped it down like hot, clear liquid and felt my
nerves sing and my skin tingle in response. I was alive
again. I had the power. There were no limits to what I
could do.

I had left the earth far behind, and still I was flying. Joy thrilled through my nerves, sang in all my senses as I left behind the boundaries of human experience. Like a night-flying bird, I soared home into blackness. The dark, throbbing energies of the universe engulfed me, filled me. I was possessed by the madness of space. Around me I heard the chorus of the stars. I was the fire at the heart of this emptiness, I was the radiance, I was the hope and the glory.

From Earth's close confines I burst into vastness, new-born. Around me: magnificence, and all possibilities. Here were my dreams, ready to come to life.

I was at home in space. It contained without constraining, moved with me like my own skin. In the throbbing, steady silence I reverberated to the music of my heart, the blood singing in my ears, the distant voices of angels, shimmering in airlessness. Being was pure bliss. There were no limitations and no laws. To think of something was to do it.

Free of restraints and illusions, I saw that the darkness was shot through with light, the silence rich with sound. The slightest motion of hand or foot sent me skimming through the vastness.

I floated past wonders and marvels. Far away, yet clearly visible, stars exploded and new worlds were born. I swam through magnificent displays of fire and light. I played the game of creation, moving stars closer to cold planets, farther from hot ones, to give life a chance. I rearranged the constellations to suit my sense of proportion. I painted symphonies in brilliant-hued gas clouds, composed poetry in lines of star-fire. A hundred times I destroyed galaxies, a hundred times startled new ones into existence. All life was a game to me.

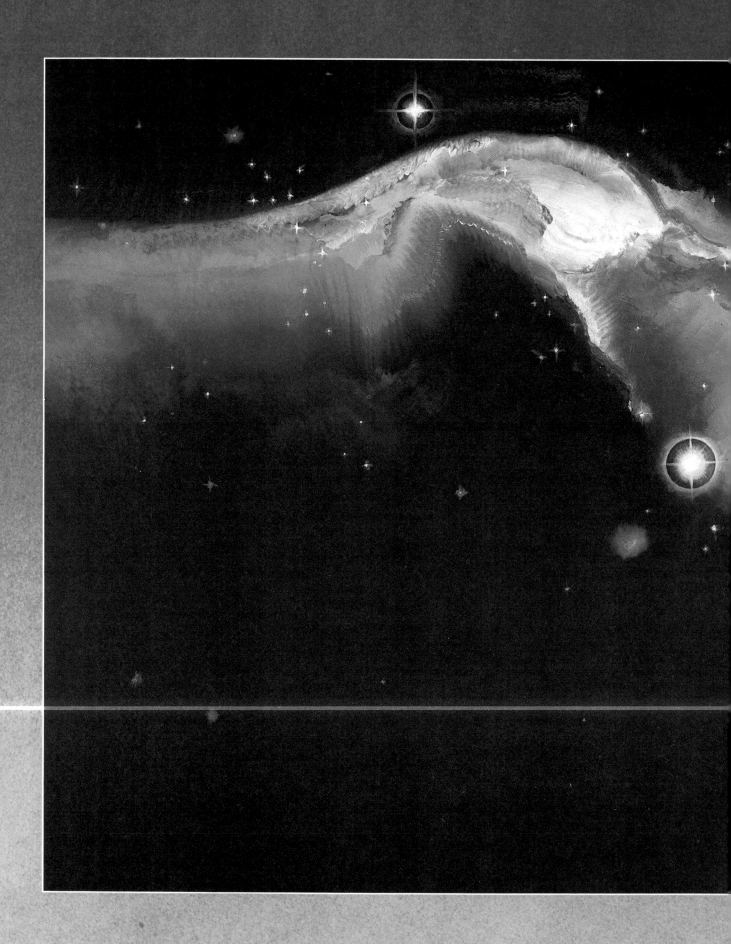

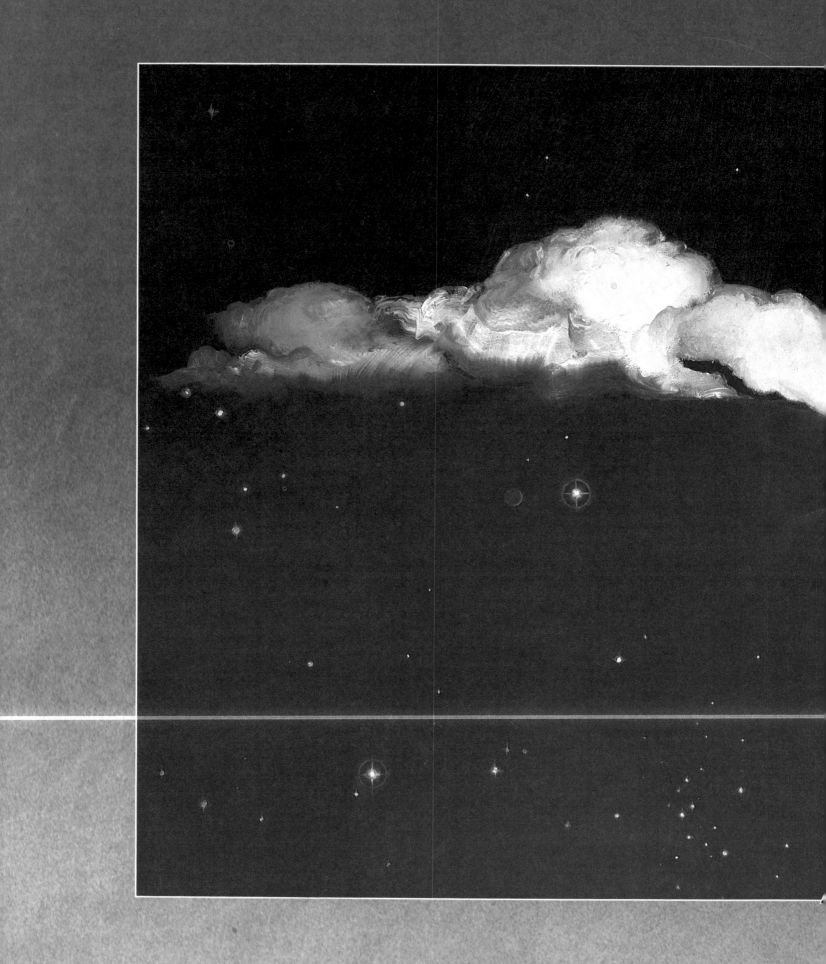

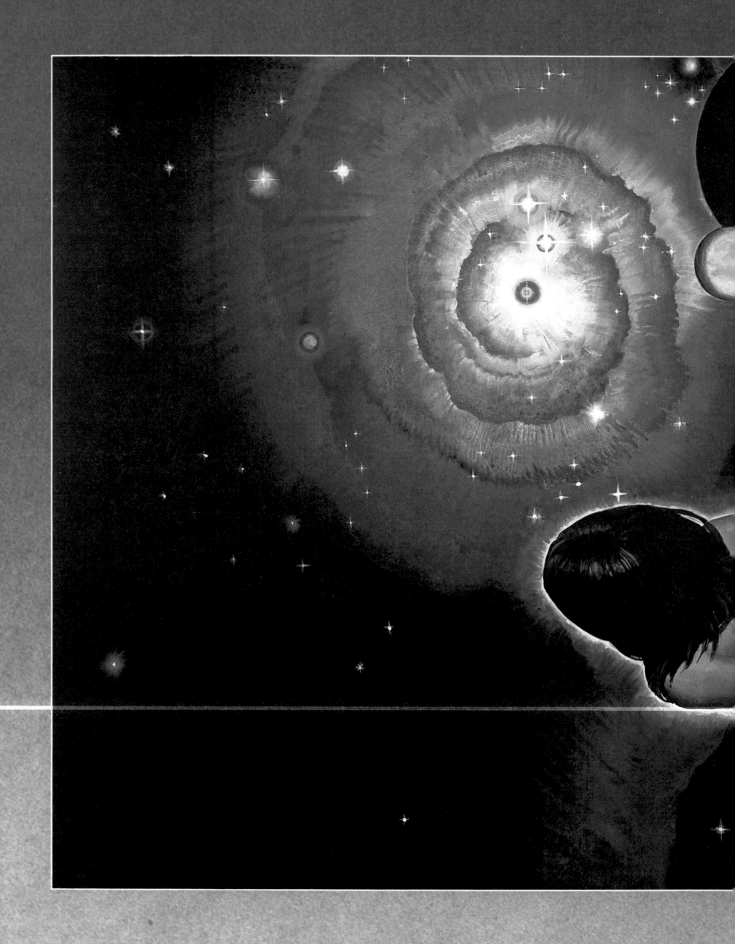

But for all my games, for all the sensual and creative joys of this existence, I was alone. And—after some unmeasured span of time—I felt lonely. Throughout the vast, starry reaches of the sky I had found no others like myself. I often thought of the angel of my childhood dreams, and sometimes it seemed I sensed a presence, hovering close to me, but for all my powers and all my searching I was still alone. The whole universe stretched before me. Where would I go? What would I do next? The choice was mine.

One particular, small, blue-green planet, shining like a semi-precious stone against black velvet, still tugged at my heart. I had been born there, had lived there, and sometimes I still felt a longing for ordinary, earthly things: the tender green grass and new pink buds of spring; the smells of woodsmoke, leaf-mould and wildflowers; the welcome, cool wetness of water on a hot day; the roar and salt-tang of the sea; the magnificent view of mountains . . . above all, the company of people, ordinary and flawed: the laughter of a child, the touch of a man's hand.

So I turned away from the boundless freedom of the universe. I decided to give up infinity and resume my life as an ordinary woman. I thought, as I made my decision, that I heard a distant sigh, a sound of omnipotent amusement at my folly, but although I waited, hoping, no word was spoken.

I hurtled back to earth like a comet, like a falling angel.

I had meant to come silently, to feel the wind in my hair and the sand between my toes in some quiet corner of the world, but this was not possible. My return caused stirrings and rumblings, wrinkles in the smooth fabric of time.

I could not hide. It was too late to pretend to be just another woman.

Thunder and lightning announced my return. There were portents when I appeared: young men saw visions, virgins gave birth, statues bled and new-born infants spoke.

In my presence the earth trembled and graves opened, disgorging the dead. Rainbows looped across the sky. I scattered miracles on the wind.

Naturally, I was worshipped. There were rituals, and offerings to encourage me to stay. Sometimes I appeared as a beautiful woman, sometimes as a milk-white mare, sometimes an owl, or an eagle, or a snake, or a cat. In all my avatars worshippers recognised my godhead, and named me, and built temples, and created explanations for my existence, invented husbands and daughters, off spring and lovers, not understanding they were all the same, all a part of Me.

My power encompassed me like a shield. At times it seemed more punishment than blessing, for I could not cast it off, and it isolated me even among crowds. I was always alone.

To those who could see, my aura marked me out as a goddess, and they worshipped in their varied ways. But others could not see me at all. I walked invisible down crowded city streets, always unnoticed.

I had not returned to earth for this loneliness, but the alternative—to accept divinity, to be worshipped as a goddess, to be set apart from my worshippers—did not satisfy me.

What was the meaning of my power? I longed to find someone who could tell me what I should do.

I remembered the angel who had visited me in my childhood. I remembered the dreams which had first stirred my discontent, which had set me on the long road to the present moment. I had found my dreams, I had heard the music of the stars for myself, and it had not been enough. Despite the ecstasy and the glory, I was still dissatisfied, still searching. Would anything ever be enough?

And then, suddenly, I knew why I had returned. I knew what I must do.

Among all the peoples of the earth there must be some who would neither fall down to worship, nor be unable to see me. There must be some who could understand. There must be others like me.

I had been found. Now it was my duty to find *them*. I would transfer the spark of curiosity, the restless, searching fire, to their souls. I would touch their hearts with the rainbow, open their eyes to wonder. I would help them transform themselves, and then I would no longer be alone.

Hope drove me, but it was more difficult than I had expected. People could not understand, or refused the gift I offered as if it were a curse. Perhaps it was. I continued to search. All time was at my disposal: I had discovered the simple, liberating truth that time was an illusion. An illusion could not bind me—I could travel as easily into the past or the future as I could walk in different directions. It was a delicious sensation, indescribable, to let myself go, slipping back through time, feeling myself infinitely receding. Sometimes the slide backwards was so exhilarating that I let myself go much too far before shooting forward again.

I dipped in and out of years, sampling people's lives, Somewhere, somewhen, I was certain I would find someone who would recognise me. But those who saw me interpreted my presence in their own ways: I was taken for the devil, a ghost, a god, a fantasy, madness, a dream, an angel . . .

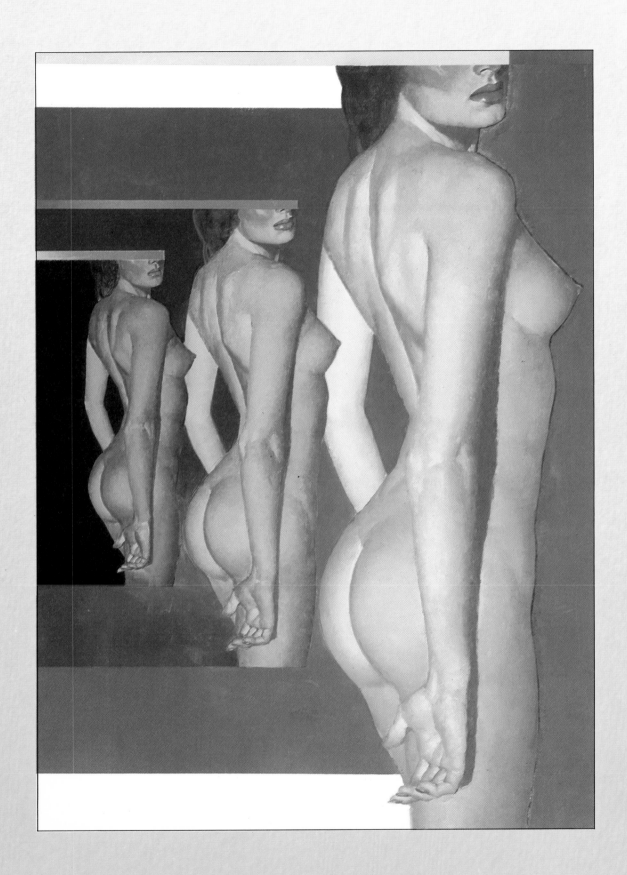

There was a little girl, fresh and innocent, so small and perfect that I felt the nearly-forgotten longing to be a mother, to bear a child of my own. I pulled her close to me, stroking her velvety-soft arms and kissing her silken hair. Sleepily, she smiled up into my face and put her arms trustingly around my neck, nuzzling into my warmth.
"Tell me a story," she commanded.
I smiled and told her about the colours of space and the voices of the stars, all the wonders that existed in the vast darkness beyond the confines of this tiny world. For her pleasure, I made up stories about palaces of jade and carnelian, ruby and emerald, hidden away in the valleys of the moon. I sang to her, and rocked her to sleep, and, briefly, I wasn't lonely.
Again and again she called me back to her. I almost forgot my quest; I could not resist her magnetism. And then one night, gazing into her face, I saw what I had somehow managed to ignore, what I must have known all along. The little girl was me.

So who was I? An angel? A dream?
The world slipped away from me. I didn't
know where I was, nor when, nor whom. It
wasn't possible. How could I be in two
places at once, both girl and goddess?
My whole life had been founded on
something that could not have happened.
There was no angel, no strange, exotic
creature from the stars, only myself.
But it had happened.
The ground beneath my feet was as resilient
and smooth as my own flesh, and for a
moment I could not tell where my body
ended and everything else began. My hair
flowed away into clouds, into the sun. I
embraced infinity. The whole world, all
being, was within me, contained by my
mortal, human body.
For a moment, I understood.

Then memory cancelled itself. I wasn't ready to understand. I fell back into the old universe, hiding my face in the veil of illusion, forgetting.

They found me in the marshes, among the tall reeds, and cleaned and dressed and married me to their king, all in accordance with some prophecy. I taught them the arts of writing and healing and farming, and in return they built massive stone temples to my glory, and gave me their most virile young men, that I should be pleased to ensure the fertility of the land. Life was easy and sweet.

At the same time, in another country, I had another name, another husband, other duties. Temples of stone were built here, too, amid the dense jungle foliage, but they were not dedicated to love. I stood at the summit surrounded by fires belching black smoke, dressed in gold and feathers, and watched, stony-eyed, as they cut out each other's hearts and offered them to me.

I breathed life into the nostrils of the dying, and wielded the sacrificial knife. I was the Great Mother, the Goddess of Love, responsible for birth and fruitfulness, and I was also the black witch, the sow who devours her young, the bird-woman who shrieks through the night to rend and tear the men who dare to love her.

From the very beginning there were gods and goddesses. Humankind needed them, created them as a way of understanding the world, a useful paradigm which, over the years, became accepted as the reality and not the image.

Images, dolls, masks, veils, illusions . . . so many different names, so many different faces, and all of them the same. Strip away the mask of civilisation and another mask appears.

They created me, giving me new names, new attributes and powers, commanding me to kill or heal. I tried to be what they wanted, and I embraced contradiction and paradox.

Deeper into the past, deeper into myself I went, into the heart of darkness, seeking the beginning, the truth behind the stories, the solid base beneath the shifting form. I turned my back on people, their demands and descriptions of me. I tried to strip away all the masks.

It was good to be alone again, to feel myself a part of nature. Sometimes, in the still of the night, drowsing with my cheek against a rock still warm from the sun, feeling the cold edge of the wind scrape my back, I thought there was no difference between me and the mountain. We were each a part of the same thing.

The idea clung to me even in daylight, when I strode along, feeling the pull of muscles in my legs, tasting dust on my tongue or sniffing the ozone tang of approaching rain. Could the rock feel as I did? Could the mountain move? Could the earth remember?

The sense of unity seemed to contradict my specific individual memories, and yet my memories contradicted themselves, for I had lived not one life but many. How was it possible?

I looked at the mountain and I was the mountain. I was the distant star beyond. I was the earth and its creator. I was the player and the game.

Had I forgotten, or only pretended to forget? Time and matter were both illusions, the oldest, most convincing mask of all, which I now reached up and peeled from my face.

The rainbow snake, the serpent of wisdom, stirred within me, and I shuddered with mixed pleasure and pain as his flaming scales seared me along the length of my spine. He had the power—*I* had the power—to set me free.

The world shimmered and dissolved. I let it go. I no longer needed to sustain the illusion. Why should I restrict myself? I had seen through the illusion. I was free.

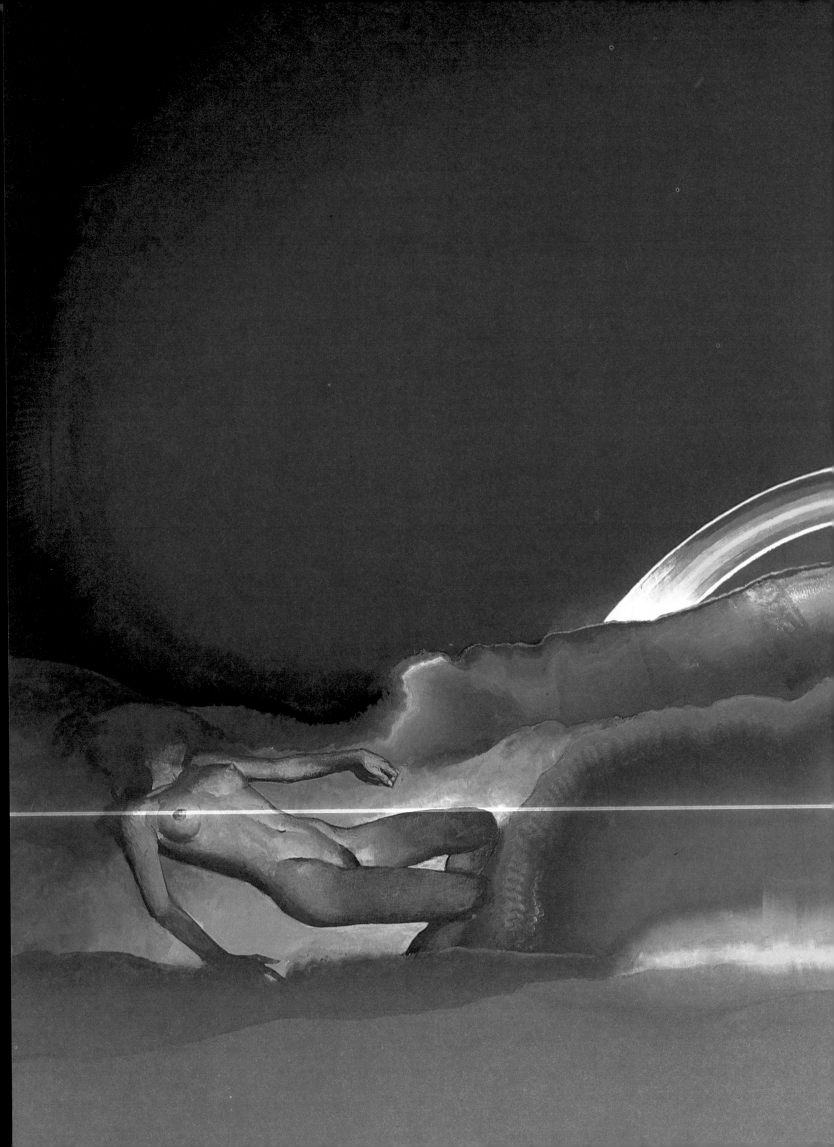

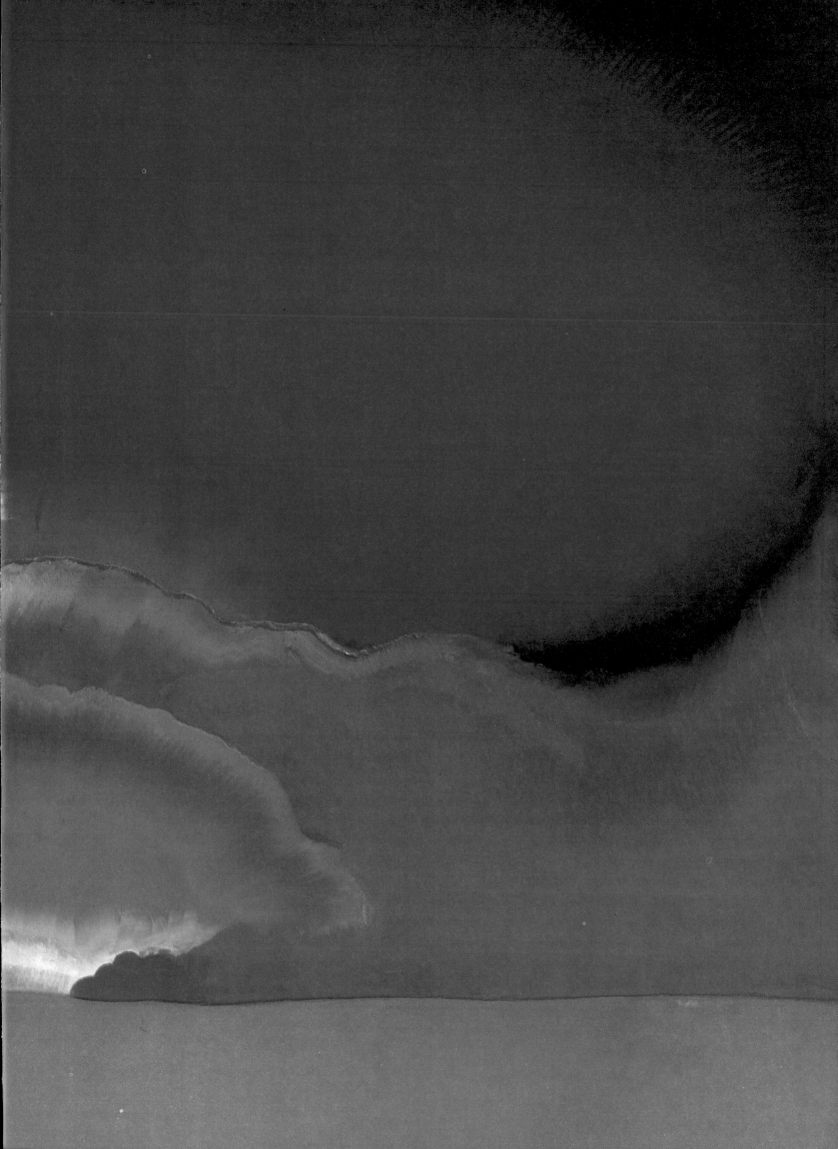

I rose, floating in a sea of memories, drifting on
clouds of sensory impressions. All my many
lifetimes, everything I had done and thought and
said clamoured within me. All the people I had
seen and known, all the places I had travelled. I
absorbed them all. I was them all. Separateness
was an illusion, a game I had played with myself.
All was one, and I was one and all. The rainbow
snake which rippled through my body with power,
also circled the world, drawing all of time and
spaced together into one unity. End and beginning
came together, indistinguishable.
My life had been a journey towards this moment of
understanding, and yet I had always known, for the
knowledge was always me, a part of me, awaiting
discovery. The world embraced me and I embraced
the world, holding it within me.
The game was over now. It was time to give up the
world, and my body with it, to vanish into nothing,
back into the void which gave me birth, to make the
circle complete.
What is nothingness? What lies beyond?
I stretch out my arms to accept the unknowable. I
give up everything, all knowledge, all illusion, all
awareness.
I was.
I am.
I shall be?
I.